My Book

Illustrated by Joanne Friar

Richard C. Owen Publishers, Inc.
Katonah, New York

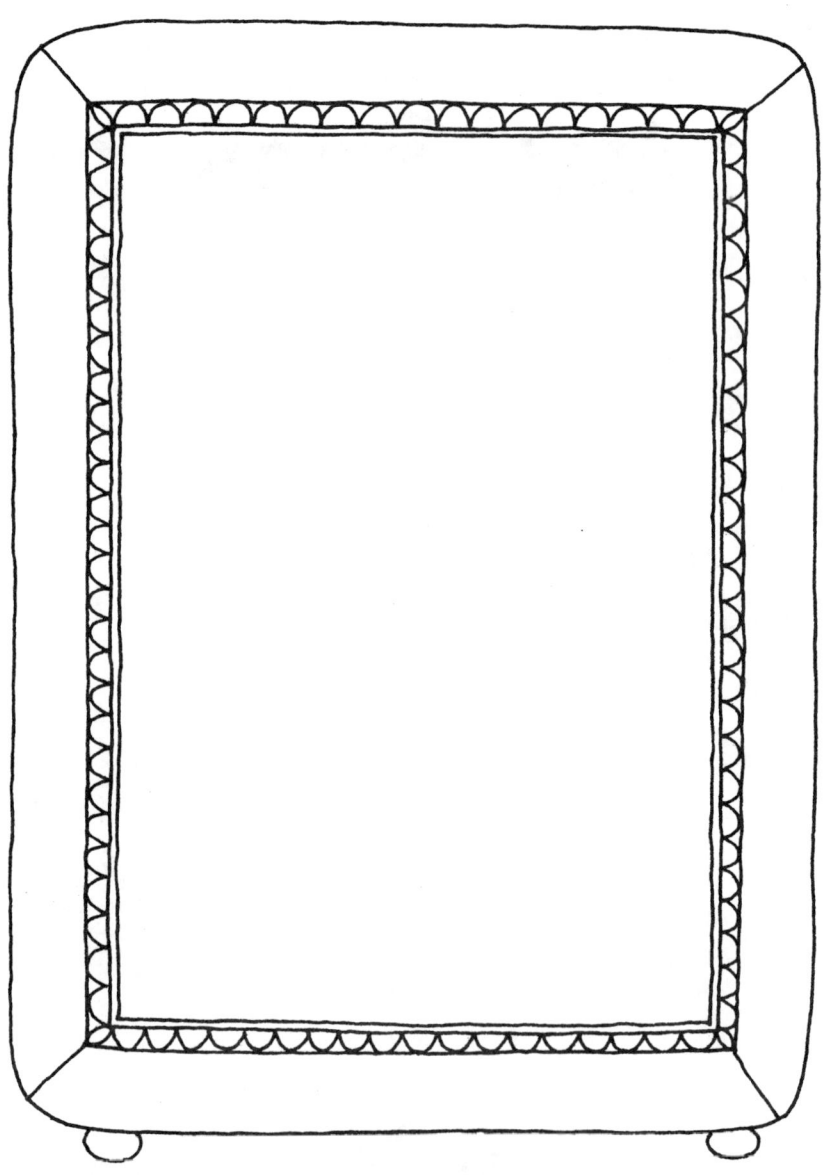

My name is _____.

I am _____ years old.

My address is _____.

My phone number is_____.

This is my family.

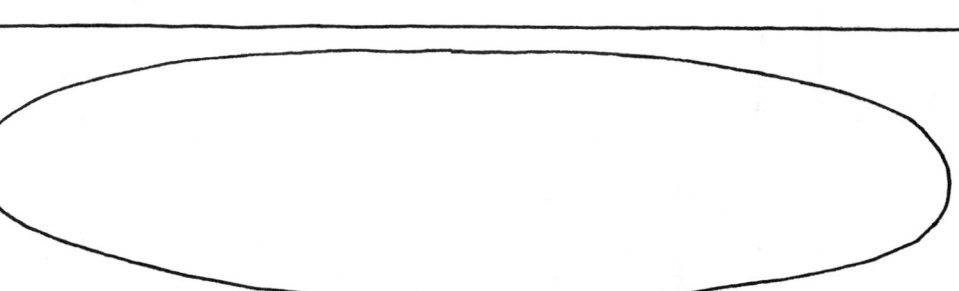

At home I like to _____.

My teacher's name is _____.

These are my friends.

One thing I like to do at school is

_____.

My favorite book is _____.